Praise for Sherri Elliott-Yeary, Bestselling Author

"In the not for profit organizational space, failure to understand, harness and accept the power of generational differences is the difference between mission success or failure. Sherri's insights are insightful and invaluable."

Paul A. Markowski, CAE
Chief Executive Officer
American Association of Clinical Endocrinologists

"*Crack the Millennial Code* provides thought-provoking realities you need to consider. It affords actionable ideas on how to gain better understanding of what drives today's workforce and marketplace to deliver exceptional results."

George Killebrew
SVP of Corporate Sponsorship
Dallas Mavericks

"I believe this is the most challenging time in our history, particularly in business, for understanding, relating to, blending and working with the different generations. Sherri Elliott-Yeary's new series: *Crack the Millennial Code* is a masterful work that not only gives an understanding of the generational differences, but also how to engage effectively with Millennials. I highly recommend *Crack the Millennial Code* to anyone in business to utilize Sherri's blueprint for generational marketing success."

Gary Barnes
President
GaryBarnesInternational.com

"I remember clearly the day I offered to pick up my niece at the airport. I told her just to call me when the plane landed. She hesitated and then asked, 'Can I just text you?' I realized she hesitated because she wasn't sure I knew how to text message and didn't want to be rude if I didn't (I did). I had to smile, though, because this intergenerational exchange was just a microcosm of what's going on in workplaces every day. Sherri Elliott-Yeary provides helpful insights into the nature of and reasons for these generational differences and offers strategies for leveraging them to an organization's advantage."

Susan R. Meisinger, SPHR
Past President
Society for Human Resource Management

"If you want results, the most important thing that any of us can do in today's ever-changing world is to truly understand the needs of the human beings we're hoping to lead or influence without judgment. Sherri's new **Crack the Millennial Code** series is an excellent resource to help any business—especially marketers—get a foundational understanding of the core needs for the 'largest generation in American History."

Kimberly Davis
Author of Brave Leadership: *Unleash Your Most Confident, Powerful, and Authentic Self to Get the Results You Need*

"If you think this book is another research book—think again. **Crack the Millennial Code** offers a direct line into the lives of this generation and explains what drives their behavior. This book isn't just for "marketers" who want to reach people, but in fact anyone who works in an office with Millennials, strives to reach a new audience, or simply wants to understand the new world of engagement that we live in today."

Dr. Alise Cortez
Engagement Coach

Crack the Millennial Code:
Strategies to Market to Millennials

Sherri Elliott-Yeary, SPHR

**Best Selling Author of Ties to Tattoos:
Turning Generational Differences into a Competitive Advantage**

Published by Generational Guru
An Imprint of Soar 2 Success Publishing
Soar2SuccessPublishing.com

ISBN: 9781949087000
Printed in the USA

Book Design by Chris Mendoza
ChrisdMendoza.com

Back Cover and Interior Headshot by Kim Ortiz Photography
KimOrtiz.com

5 Generational Images by Michaels Wilder Agency
Sherri Elliott-Yeary, LLC

Bulk discounts available.
For details visit **www.GenerationalGuru.com**
or contact Sherri Elliott-Yeary at 469-971-3663
or **Sherri@GenerationalGuru.com**

Dedication

"Any job very well done that has been carried out by a person who is fully dedicated is always a source of inspiration."

Carlos Ghosn

This book is dedicated to the amazing Millennial ladies in my life. They encourage me to be open to change and to think outside of the box.

I am also grateful to my granddaughter Aubrey who reminds her Grams that life is meant to be FUN and I should never forget to play like I am five years old from time to time!

Thank you to my husband Manny for encouraging me to take on this important and timely project.

Most of all, thank you to my readers who support and encourage me to continue writing on the importance of generational diversity and inclusion.

TABLE OF CONTENTS

Chapter One

Why Millennials Matter Now

"If the whole world depends on today's youth, I can't see the world lasting another 100 years."

– Socrates 2400 years ago

Millions of people around the globe watched live with bated breath as the US Congress grilled for two days one of the world's most influential Millennials about the horrors of "too much" technology. There were 44 graying senators against one young man. The media expected Mark Zuckerberg (born 1984) to get deep fried and burned beyond recognition. Yet instead of persecution, on a curious turn of events – he was unscathed. What initially started as a PR nightmare for his behemoth social media company resulted in a Facebook stock price increase of 4.5% that same day.

Apparently, the government can no longer suppress the digital revolution just like parents can't hold back their kids from coming of age. The world is on the verge of another eon, there's no denying that.

The poles are literally shifting beneath our feet. Lobbying power, influence, voting rights and money are changing hands from the old to the young. That means there's no turning back. You and I can't turn back the clock. In this time and age, we have to adapt, or we'll go obsolete like a 1998 dial-up internet connection.

Millennials are now outgrowing their fragile snowflake, social media obsessed image. In between securing their first full-time job and trying to pay off their enormous student loans, they are already defining trends and disrupting markets. We should realize by this time that pigeonholing this young group of people into boxes labeled as entitled, narcissistic, self-interested, unfocused, and lazy is the ultimate form of "old generation shortsightedness." Interestingly, those exact adjectives were also hurled by the Traditionalist Generation to the Baby Boomers.

Let's move past this juvenoia cycle so we can focus on the things that really matter.

Throughout mankind's history, new fads always scare the old and excite the young. These days they say that technology distracts and "dumbs down" the Millennial generation. No wonder, even Socrates back in his days believed that writing thoughts on paper (or parchment) will eventually "dumb down" young people.

Fast forward to the next decade: the Millennials will complain about how the Gen Z teens won't even leave their rooms and go back to "reality," immersed all day in their own virtual world as projected on glasses and contact lenses. Two more generations from now, we'll achieve hyper-connectedness with the world's internet network embedded right under our skin and in our devices.

Technology is changing at an exponential rate. What we see our young people doing are adaptive behaviors in line with the changing times.

The only way to move and make money in this digital age is to shift our generational perspective – and that's exactly what this book is all about.

In the next few chapters of this book, I will share actionable strategies you can use to help **Crack the Millennial Code**. It's my goal to make them simple so you can apply them immediately.

Who Am I and What Do I Know About Marketing to Millennials?

What makes me the person to provide the key to unlocking the myths surrounding this generation? My personal exploration of how generational paradigms influence leadership and family began in early childhood. When I was eight years old, I remember overhearing my mom and our neighbor crying hysterically. They had just heard on the radio that Elvis Presley had died. To an eight-year-old, this made no sense. Why were they so upset, and who was this Elvis guy anyway?

While people of all ages simultaneously experience large-scale events similar to the loss of a cultural icon like Elvis, it is the younger people who are in the value-forming stages that are most likely to be significantly shaped by them, which is why these events can have such a powerful impact. My mom and neighbor were grief-stricken, and I learned that Elvis was a significant person even though I didn't know who he was.

The realization of the way significant events shape the values of the different generations became solidified when I attended university and took a psychology class that ultimately changed the course of my life.

One day, the psychology professor showed the class a video featuring Morris Massey, author of *The People Puzzle*. He said that the first 10 years of a person's life are the most critical years because this is when the individual's values, beliefs, and attitudes are shaped. These crucial years include defining moments such as historical or political events, the financial climate, and popular culture like Elvis Presley.

Morris Massey found that a high percentage of learned behaviors and attitude patterns in adults are directly correlated to their formative years. According to Massey, the major factors influencing value development are:

- Family and friends
- Media
- Formal and informal education
- Church & religion
- Income
- Geography
- Teachers, formal and informal

I found the idea of formative influences so fascinating that I became actively involved in generational studies. I eventually went on to research, train, consult, and address organizations on the topic of generational differences to assist them with improving productivity, gaining a larger share in the marketplace, and developing a better workplace culture to cultivate and retain top talent.

Through this work, it became apparent to me that a framework was needed in which the power of understanding and acceptance of generational differences could be harnessed and put to productive use in the workplace and in our families.

At Generational Guru, I decided to embark on a comprehensive research project — interviewing and surveying hundreds of working people across the country in a wide range of industries and of varying ages and experience levels. We've studied corporate culture at the request of many Fortune 500 brands. Following the completion of these research projects, I shared our findings in my first book, *Ties to Tattoos: Turning Generational Differences into a Competitive Advantage*, in 2009, with the second edition in 2015.

As this concept continues to grow in popularity, I am frequently asked to speak to marketing teams about how to reach the various generations as clients, customers, and consumers. The findings from this long-conducted research is what you're reading today in this book.

Many of my clients' stories and genuine struggles are included here. To maintain anonymity for all who shared their thoughts and opinions, their names have been changed to honor their brave contributions. You may recognize some of these challenges and personalities in your own workplace and marketplace.

The American writer Carl Sandburg once said, "Nothing happens unless first a dream." In today's digital world, many Internet marketers and audience development professionals would paraphrase this differently by saying, "Nothing happens unless engagement exists."

The **Crack the Millennial Code** series is intended to be an insightful tool to help you harness the power of the largest and most influential generation — Millennials.

Crack the Millennial Code: Strategies to Market to Millennials is about showing you how to create engagement with the most significant generation of consumers in American history.

Chapter Two

The Millennial Genesis

"The only people to whose opinions I listen to now with any respect are people much younger than myself. They seem in front of me. Life has revealed to them her latest wonder."
— Oscar Wilde, the Picture of Dorian Gray

The best way to decode the Millennial mind is to understand the state of the world during their coming of age, a time that strangely coincides with the birth of a new era. Unlike the New Year, the beginning of an epoch isn't marked by loud bangs or fireworks. Like a frog in hot water, we have never seen the changes coming, not until it's over. Previously, the beginning of a cultural revolution began during man's discovery of fire, then by the birth of the steam engine, and finally during the first spark of the electric current. On a curious turn of events, the time when Millennials entered adulthood were also the years of economic death – and the birth of a new way of life.

For two centuries, older generations were depleting the earth of its scarce resources, fueling their farms, factories, and cars. In July 2008, gasoline prices peaked at a record high. Sixty days later, the stock market came crashing down. Our decades of blind dependence on fossil fuels backfired. The outdated financial and capitalist system couldn't hold it any longer.

The big bubble burst, the coffers had gone dry, and millions of middle-class families worldwide plunged into poverty and despair. After decades of abundance, the government finally failed us. Like a mother who abandoned her kids in the dead of winter, the central banks flushed our safety net of money and our kid's futures down the drain. In between all that rush and madness, a new age of hyper-connectedness and sustainable energy was born.

Straight out of college, Millennials were thrust into that chaos-filled world. They saw businesses going bankrupt, houses repossessed, and their parents being laid off. Due to the massive betrayal of trust and uncertainty, the Millennials became cynics who despise authority.

#YOLO (which means You Only Live Once) best describes the Millennial mindset. They say so because they have seen how careers and objects that their parents devoted their whole lives to could evaporate into thin air. They watched as the life in their parents' faces dissipated over decades while toiling at their 9 to 5 jobs. All these years, older generations were putting off that dream vacation, giving away their four decades of freedom to pay off mortgages. So, unlike their self-sacrificing Boomer parents, Millennials realize that they must live now, not tomorrow, and not in the future.

Despite being cash-strapped, they are twice more likely to travel than older generations. Interestingly, their sense of adventure isn't a one season thing. More and more Millennials are quitting their corporate jobs to pursue a nomad lifestyle. Nowadays, it's no longer about who earns more, but about who's living "the life." In this time and age, meaning and impact have become their currency.

Today, Millennials are trading security for freedom. These young people are slowly erasing the borders that define their citizenship, race, religion and even gender.

One of the best examples of this type of Millennial is Harvard-educated Palestinian, Nuseir Yassin (born 1992). He is a top Facebook influencer more popularly known as Nas Daily. He's traveling to a different country every week while filming his adventures for the world to see in real time. This young guy's optimism is something else entirely. It's no wonder he's already amassed a record of 800 million views and counting for his one-minute Facebook videos.

Even giving birth and having babies won't slow down their wanderlust. Just look at Filipino-American Garrett Gee (born 1989) who co-founded and cashed in millions for his app called Scan during its Snapchat acquisition. He left his cushy startup millionaire lifestyle, sold all their belongings and then decided to go backpacking all over the world with his wife and three babies.

Unconsciously, they perceive that there's no point in delaying gratification when everything can be gone at any time. So, don't be so quick to label them narcissistic if they choose to take a hundred selfies and record everything they do on Facebook Live. They have to capture every fleeting moment while it lasts. They also know that selfies get higher engagement, which means more eyeballs and traffic. Nope, it's not the kind of traffic where you get stuck, but the traffic superhighway to more likes, followers, and ultimately, into passive Internet income.

About half of Millennials are underemployed, considering that they are the most educated of any other generation. Their college tuition fees ballooned to five times more than their parents during their time. Based on their meager minimum salaries, it will take them at least 30 years to pay off their combined college and personal debts.

As a result, they are sacrificing breakfast. They are the people who popularize brunch. So, if they choose to take a picture of their nice meal, let them be. We thought food was a necessity, but for them, a nice healthy meal is a luxury – something to be savored and shared with their thousands of peers before it's gone.

Millennials are also the least trusting and the most skeptical about traditional powers. Just take a look at their outlaw whistleblowers, who were both despised by Boomers yet idolized by Millennials — Edward Snowden (born 1983) and Chelsea Manning (born 1987).

The bombing of the Twin Towers marked the start of the day when they'll never feel safe, even on their own soil. Likewise, witnessing the war on terror and the abandoned shell-shocked kids in real time, as reported by all the major news outlets, made them sympathetic to these people, regardless of color or nationality.

The birth of the first blockchain money, Bitcoin, started as an idea around October 2008 during the deepest pit of recession. Interestingly, the motivation behind the creation of the blockchain technology mirrors the drivers of Millennial psychology.

This recent technology revolves around the principle of transparency, stability, decentralization, removal of the governing authority and democratization of money – values that our century-old system desperately lacks. That might also be the reason why Millennials rally around cryptocurrency like bees to honey.

Chapter Three

The Components of the Millennial Code

"We can't solve problems by using the same kind of thinking we used when we created them."

– Albert Einstein

How fast can you create a billion dollars? For generations, we believed that you needed to work really hard for decades to be super rich. Just ask Warren Buffett (born 1930) who got his first billion dollars after years of toil at the ripe age of 56. Similarly, Carlos Slim acquired his first billion at age 51 while Larry Ellison isn't far behind at age 49. These men are the Traditionalists who experienced first-hand the devastation of World War II. The next generation, Boomers, followed the same wealth trajectory as Oprah, who made her first billion at age 49, and Sir Richard Branson, who attained his rebel billionaire status at 41. Gen Xers such as Elon Musk similarly became a billionaire at age 41, while Jeff Bezos hit the same billionaire status at age 35.

Since 1987, only one person holds the record as the youngest self-made billionaire ever — Bill Gates at 31. Like Roger Bannister breaking the 4-minute-mile and human speed limit barriers during the 1952 Olympics, it was estimated that it would take another two decades to break that "wealth speed record."

Mark Zuckerberg (born 1984) and Evan Spiegel (born 1990) broke that billion-dollar speed limit just this decade. Zuckerberg, the CEO of Facebook and Instagram, earned his first billion at age 23 while Spiegel attained his self-made billionaire status at age 25, transitioning from dorm room founders to social media magnates at warp speed.

And just when you think Mark Zuckerberg's record will be the billion-dollar barrier for this generation, businesswoman and social media influencer Kylie Jenner hit her 900 million mark at age 20, just halfway into 2018. Some may see these Millennials as entitled, unfocused and lazy, but these numbers tell a different story, and they are just warming up.

Who are Millennials?

At Generational Guru, we've been in the "Millennial" business for a decade and *"Who are Millennials?"* is still the most common question we're asked.

Statisticians will tell you Millennials are young adults born after 1980. There are more than 80 million of them living in the United States today, and they are quickly outnumbering the Boomers as the most significant generation in the US and worldwide population. They are already gaining steam with a direct spending power of over $65 billion each year – more than Boomers or Gen X. They populate over a quarter of the globe and are set to dominate politics and the corporate landscape for decades to come.

Small and large businesses alike will benefit greatly once they understand how to "decode" these young buyers. Now, as a business owner or marketer, you might say, "But we aren't Google or Facebook or Apple. We don't have the budget to accommodate six-figure annual salaries, exotic beach soirees, or free cafeteria food for life! We are a small business. We can't do major million-dollar ad campaigns!"

Yes, that I know. You use elevators, not adult slides. You don't sit on bean bags or do napping pods. You would like to maximize returns for every penny spent. That being said: Can you market your company as a Millennial-preferred brand and workplace without running out of cash? Can you recalibrate your "make more money" mission to entice brilliant Millennial minds? Can you tweak your branding to make these young people go raving mad about your product? Yes, you can. I'll tell you how in the following chapters.

The Millennial Persona

Millennials aren't a homogenous group. They share the same need to find meaning yet their interpretation of this "meaning" differs. Collectively and individually, they want to make an impact; however, they do it in a thousand different ways. So, to make our jobs as business owners and marketers easier, we at Generational Guru endeavored to classify the persona that is dominant in this young group of people.

Since Millennials aren't all the same, your first step is to identify who they are and what makes them tick.

1. The Hero

They are the loudest social media influencers. These young people typically use strong expressions to speak of something they are passionate about. They are relentless and driven by their hobbies or cause. They are gregarious, open to change, and have an enviable magnetic personality.

The hero Millennial refuses to follow the norm, goes on a journey of self-discovery, details their ordeals and challenges followers to be altruists and rule-breakers — all the while posting tales of conquest on Facebook, Medium, YouTube, or on their own blog. Adidas' "Impossible is Nothing" and Nike's "Find your Greatness" taps into the hero persona inside every young person. Millennials love games such as League of Legends, Warcraft, and Clash of Clans because it taps into their desire for conquest and triumph.

Tip:

Get your hero Millennials to rally behind your cause by creating a leaderboard. Give them small tasks acting as "milestones." Let them compete against each other at every step. Offer them recognition as it happens. Make your leaderboard visible on your website's Home page or showcase it at your office on a big-screen TV. It would be best if you could connect it to the Internet, so the leaderboard updates itself in real time.

Millennials love instant recognition. Leaderboards can give them constant minute-by-minute feedback. Think about displaying your competition like a CrossFit® "box," where your results are posted at the end of the workout, so everyone can gather around and take a selfie.

2. The Wanderlust

Ask anybody below age 30 about his/her ultimate life goal and more than half will say that they want to see the world. This type of travel is unlike anything experienced by prior generations.

First, they prefer not to spend their hard-earned money at fancy hotels. They prefer Airbnb and other types of smaller lodging accommodations with a comfortable local setting. Second, they rarely have a fixed itinerary and are more apt to go with the flow. These surfer bods, boho chicks, and mountain dudes love to take pictures with local kids, exotic street foods, crimson sunsets, mountain peaks and beach waves.

Tip:

Awaken your Millennial customers' wanderlust gene by giving them a "passport" complete with a "treasure map" for your season's exclusive campaign. If you want to cash in to this persona all year long, recreate your brand or your office as a laid-back community. Ask these young people about their version of "paradise" and recreate your theme and your office building according to how they see their happy place.

3. The Activist

Millennials nowadays aren't afraid to proudly step out of the closet. They transcend gender stereotypes and overcome mental health stigma without fear of judgment. They are also the least prejudiced and most tolerant among all generations alive right now. The *#MeToo* movement that shook Hollywood wouldn't have gone viral if not for Millennial hashtag warriors on Twitter, Facebook, Instagram and YouTube.

At this time and age, Millennials have the highest energy and the most resources to pursue their causes – more so than any other generation. Boomers are too busy climbing the corporate ladder and trying to pay off their mortgage while Gen Z's are still in school, so both couldn't care less.

Social media websites cashed in on last year's rainbow LGBTQ movement by encouraging self-expression without bias. Facebook and Instagram released picture effects allowing users to show their support for "gay pride." This engagement tactic can be done by users at a click of a button.

Tip:

Whether you have a local or an international event coming up, you can start "trending" by asking Millennials for support. Start with a compelling and emotional short article and encourage Millennials to share it on their timelines.

Think of a catchy hashtag to go along with your event, contest, business, or cause such as #ContestEntry #WinItWednesday #Paleo #GenerationalGuru (my brand) or #[your brand name] with a popular extension by linking to an influential person who may use your product.

Find out about your Millennial market's enemy or pet peeves. Lure them into action. Encourage them to "throw rocks" at the people and issues that make them angry. No need for sticks and stones; a few hashtag barrages will do. Treat them as an equal. Rally behind them to make them loyal to your brand.

4. The Boss

If the hero persona is typically male, the Millennial "boss babes" are their female equivalent. Women are now outnumbering men on the college grounds. They are more likely to live independently outside their parent's homes after graduation. They usually hold a leadership position at work or are founders of their own businesses.

These young women are conscious about their image, insanely driven and are vulnerable at the same time. They have a massive reserve of energy and social influence. They are crushing the day for all its worth, juggling gym time, work, and socializing with friends without slowing down unless it's to grab their favorite Kombucha.

Apparently, they have more spending power than their

counterparts. Research shows that women without children are more likely to spend more on personal care, groceries and household products. They aren't afraid to splurge and invest in high-quality brands that help them live a lavish lifestyle.

Tip:

Don't stereotype these women. They might seem materialistic, but they don't want to be treated as such. There are a lot of causes that they genuinely care about. More than half of these women buy a brand's personality over the actual product.

Know their soft buttons, insecurities, and aspirations. The Dove soap campaign capitalizes on an ordinary woman's appearance in all its commercials, with the ultimate message that beauty is more than skin deep. This brand is humble yet driven, as evidenced by how they tapped into the power of accomplished young businesswomen as local brand ambassadors and spokespersons.

5.   The Broke

For these "kids," the struggle is indeed real. They like to experience and immerse themselves with what's in but might not want to pay for it. It will take them years to transition from "adulting" to an adult. They are burdened with college debt that will take them three decades to pay off. They are working but can hardly pay rent. No wonder they returned to their parents' house. They do "Netflix and chill" with a beer

or two in between their multiple part-time jobs. Most of what media and other journalists thought of as "Millennials" fall into this class. They are hanging out everywhere, so others erroneously assumed that all Millennials are adult children who still live with their parents, binge-watching the latest streaming series. Yet as you can see, they are just one small slice out of the whole Millennial pie.

Tip:

Broke Millennials are the best sale hunters and coupon clippers. They take pride in scoring great deals that are a "steal." They might not have much purchasing power, but your business can capitalize on their social media followers.

Create an affiliate program where they can refer their friends to your store or website. In return, you can offer them loyalty points they can later convert into vouchers or even cash. You can also give them a full-sized sample of your product in exchange for their reviews.

6.   The Gamer

These Millennials started playing Super Mario and Nintendo even before they could write their names. Now they are already nearing 30 years but are kids at heart. They are self-confessed regular guys, nerds, geeks and sports fanatics who see life as a big virtual reality game full of challenges and trophies. They are joyful, carefree and laid-back.

Most of them are still struggling financially, but they see to it that they have enough money for the latest high-tech gadgets, event tickets, and game upgrades. These young people are the backbone of every department, willing to do the job even without the need for acknowledgment and recognition. They're also not as vocal on social media. They prefer to be the lurkers and observers.

They like to work hard and play harder. To know more about how this Millennial gamer persona thinks, just watch the world's number one Youtuber, Felix Kjellberg (born 1989), popularly known as PewDiePie. He rarely shaves, he curses a lot, he likes to poke fun at himself and make people laugh. He treats his millions of followers as equals and calls them "bros." PewDiePie is one the best masters of the art of "selling without sounding salesy" because it hardly looks like he is endorsing anything, yet he does.

Tip:

Gamification is one of the best marketing strategies you can use to tap into this Millennial gamer generation. Your company can simulate the experience of being a customer by designing a virtual game that looks and feels exactly like the real world.

The US military is heavily into gamification as a tool to recruit and train young people. Managers can structure their routine work tasks into a series of games. Instead of the usual department, group your young employees into "teams." Give them points after accomplishing desirable behaviors. Let them advance to the "next level" and give them badges after achieving a target or a quota.

7. The Artist

Top Instagram influencers who spearhead the next trends are the Millennial artists, visionaries, and creators. Some of them have a broader fan base than Hollywood stars. They want to be seen as exceptional and authentic. Brands and young people love the artist because they are insanely creative and typically appeal to a wide variety of consumers. Top influencers know that to be endearing to their followers they must be seen as imperfect, genuine and vulnerable. Aside from selfies, they also write long-form posts that show their flaws and softer side.

These traits are the reason why older generations see them as melodramatic, narcissistic and entitled. Artists are afraid of mediocrity and conformity. This generation is also the most difficult to please as well as the most vocal about their buying experience. Most Millennials that do business on Pinterest and Etsy are of this type. They likewise love to rant on Reddit and blog on Medium.

Tip:

The fastest way to propel an unknown brand into the Millennial hive-like mind is to get an influencer to share, tag, endorse and use your product or service. Marketers and business owners must always remember that a single well-meaning picture is worth a thousand words.

Likewise, a unique video is worth a hundred pictures. No need to get a studio to shoot the perfect photo or video. Millennials want authenticity. They want to buy things but don't want to get sold. Posts that look like blatant ads get the lowest engagement. Millennials are loyal to brands and companies who know them and care about them genuinely. They want to see themselves in the picture.

Convert Millennials to your brand and philosophy by creating a mixture of credibility, vulnerability, and show them the **WIIFM** factor (What's In It For Me).

Chapter Four

Crack the Code:
Identifying Your Millennial Marketing Mix

"The best marketing doesn't feel like marketing."
— Tom Fishburne

1. Get trending.

2. Go viral.

3. Break the Internet.

These are the three stages of your Millennial marketing effectiveness.

Millennials are complex creatures. Depending on your product and market, there are a thousand different ways to their hearts and wallets. It's hard, maybe even impossible, to develop a marketing strategy for a generation you don't understand.

Unfortunately, there's not a stand-alone resource that provides all the answers. It's really an invasion that has taken many by surprise, but while the birth of 78 million babies is enormous, it did take place more than two decades ago. However, it's been so incremental that many of us have not noticed the impact. But now they are here. About half of them have already entered the workforce, the other half is not far behind, and they're bringing changes wherever they go. Their influence will only continue to grow and become more persuasive.

Every brand wants to charm Millennials. But the first trick in garnering their loyalty involves getting their attention. . . and keeping it. That's no small feat considering these younger consumers aren't as likely as Gen-Xers and Baby Boomers to respond to traditional advertising or marketing tactics.

Below is a compilation of the results of our research and the insight of more than two dozen marketing experts and executives who believe they've found the secrets to engaging with Millennials under the age of 35.

Millennials expect to feel connected to the brand before they buy.

Make Millennials Matter
+
What Matters to Millennials
=
Cracking the Code

To get you started, here are actionable tips and strategies to tap into this massive Millennial market.

1. Use big data to find out what makes them tick

One of the best ways to find out your Millennial market's interest is to look into their search history. You can use analytics and keyword research tools to find out the words and phrases that people are using in their Google searches. Facebook is also a great tool if you want to narrow them down according to age, gender, location, and interests. Create your content around these trending buzzwords.

2. Chatbots

Millennials and telemarketers don't mix. The best way to get them is through text. Talking will be the last option when text, email, and social media fail. You can't text and respond to a thousand Millennials all at once unless you have an extensive chat support system but thanks to the chatbot, companies can now send automated texts and automated interactions in real time. Find your brand's tone of voice that works for your Millennial audience and use the same for your chatbots.

More and more companies are now using **Chatbots** to speed up their customer communication processes. Want to order pizza? Get motivational quotes? Latest movie schedules? E-Commerce product feedback, returns handling, and questions? Finding the ideal clothing style according to your body shape and personality? Personal financial advice? There's a chatbot for all of these. One interesting chatbot that uses canned psychotherapy responses plus artificial intelligence is **woebot.io**. Millennials love how this CBT (Cognitive Behavioral Therapy) bot helps them during days when they feel down or anxious.

Chatbots can satisfy Millennials' need for instant feedback and constant brand communication. Unlike conventional call centers, installing a chatbot will only cost you a few dollars to set up and maintain all year long.

3. Empower and inspire

Millennials intuitively know that they have the power to change the world. Their feedback and purchasing power steers products and trends. Position your product in a way that helps them realize their full potential. Think bigger. What might be a simple app or software can be branded as a tool that will save them time, allowing them more freedom to pursue their more significant cause. Millennials aren't content with achieving independence, prominence, or financial abundance. Their need is to discover their purpose, make an impact, and find meaning that speaks to their innate desire for self-actualization.

4. Utilize various communication methods

When communicating with other people, Millennials are likely to prefer these methods (in order of importance):

- Text and IM apps, like WhatsApp and Facebook Messenger
- Social media (Facebook, Snapchat, Instagram, Twitter, Pinterest)
- Email, with the subject line being a highly important aspect
- Phone calls
- In person

These methods should be kept in mind when communicating with your Millennial market, especially when it comes to customer support. Millennials expect an instant response from brands. Millennials will ask questions on Twitter, Facebook and Instagram. If your organization has social media pages, be prepared to monitor them. Brands must respond quickly to connect the consumer to your brand. Proven studies support the fact that organizations who embrace and engage this marketing strategy will reap substantial increases in sales from those they interact with on social media platforms.

5. Allow customer participation

So, you don't have enough money to get models for your products? How about giving away discounts in exchange for pictures of your customers as they use the product? You can also turn it into a social media contest (a race to getting more likes or shares or views) to add gasoline to the fire. Millennials love brands that reflect how they want to look and how they like to portray themselves *IRL* (In Real Life) and on social media. Aside from photos, encourage your customers to post stories, videos and product reviews.

Let your target market be your star. This generation of consumers likes to see people who are like them in the media they consume. Check out Eloquii and Versona, where on-the-street customers and fashion bloggers, not models, are pictured wearing their purchases. This is a strategy you can use to instantly get social credibility plus tap into their *#FOMO* (Fear Of Missing Out). It's like hitting two birds with one stone.

6. Build your online reputation

Research shows that Millennials are more likely to do their own research online about a product or service before buying them for the first time. If your business has zero online presence, then you are surely missing out. Likewise, they'll find it hard to trust you unless you have honest customer reviews. **According to HubSpot, 84 percent of consumers research online, and 70 percent read online reviews before buying online.** Millennials are no different. They want to know from their influencers and peers that a brand is worth their loyalty and business. Commitment is hard to win, but if your brand has fans that are also influencers, you will attract Millennial consumers. If you really want to reach your target market, develop your own cool App.

7. Tap Millennial influencers

Leverage influencers' large social media following by getting them to endorse your product. The ideal influencer knows how to put the product naturally into the picture without blatant selling. Think of Tom Cruise's Top Gun and Ray-Ban aviator shades. Don't overpromise. Include product benefit comparisons and be genuine about your product's flaws. **WALK THE TALK.**

Case in point: Many cosmetics companies partner with influencers and create content based around helping their niche audience with makeup-related problems. This content might include information about how to contour cheekbones with makeup based on face shape. Another example would be a page dedicated to selling clothes online that shares tips on what outfits look best with different body shapes and sizes, or how specific articles of clothing can be styled in various ways for different occasions. This method allows you to provide expert advice to your Millennial audience while selling to them at the same time.

8. Optimize your site for mobile experience

Millennials are into fast-paced living. Most of them are more likely to shop, socialize, pay bills and work on their mobile phones. Remember, the majority of Millennials process information around them through visuals and emotions. That would be because a human brain processes images a thousand times faster than written text. Influencers love to put selfies together with their Facebook posts because data shows this type of content receives 53 percent more likes and twice the number of comments than a purely text-based post. Optimize your website and social media posts so texts and images are easy to view and not distorted on all screen sizes. Go for shareable and visible stories using real pictures, videos, and infographics.

9. Keep it brief

Don't assume Millennials are waiting around to watch long videos because they're not. One minute is the ideal video length for Facebook. For YouTube, you can go as long as ten minutes. Be sure to put in subtitles [or captioning] as over half of Millennials watch their Facebook and YouTube videos with the sound off.

Millennials are busy and always shifting from one activity to another. Trying to hold them longer than they want will bore them and will render your marketing useless. This is not to say, however, that they have an attention-deficit disorder – after all, this is the generation that will binge-watch multiple seasons of The Walking Dead in a few days' time. This just emphasizes the fact that **Millennials will only pay attention to what interests them.**

10. Be the expert

Being the expert who has the solutions to their problems will allow you to develop a relationship with this generation and will ultimately make you a trustworthy business in their minds. To do this, research what types of problems Millennials encounter that you can address firsthand, then create content about it. These methods allow you to establish yourself as a person they can approach when they have questions, and they will remember you in the future.

11. Embrace diversity

Because Millennials are authentic, forward thinkers, and risk-takers, they want the same from their products and services. Restaurants and brands should continuously be looking for new and diverse ethnic flavors as well as new ways to prepare standard ingredients. Give them a wide range of choices.

Brands can employ diversity when they focus on the values of this new generation of women and understand that they value real and honest opinions of peers and influencers more than communications from brands. As a result, marketers are shifting their focus to messages of honest opinions. That kind of thinking carries so much weight with your Millennial consumers. A good example is Dove's "Choose Beauty" campaign. This video campaign became a viral hit after people were left with different emotions while watching women of all sizes, colors, and ages make a choice. People are sharing their opinions on the impact and significance of this campaign on female empowerment.

12. Frugality

"Millennial shoppers are more heavily influenced by a range of money-saving opportunities versus the population as a whole," according to the *SymphonyIRI* report. More than half of Millennials use shopper loyalty discounts as well as traditional coupons.

Most Millennials are willing to go out of their way to go to a brick and mortar store versus online if the retailer offers an attractive reward program. Costco, for example, offers discounted gift cards to movies, restaurants, etc., which results in approximately 20 percent savings from regular prices. When you sign up as a Gold Executive member, you earn an annual 2 percent reward up to $1,000 based on your prior year's purchases. This is precisely what Millennials want – value and savings. Meanwhile, Costco is getting what they want – a connection to their brand.

Millennials are interested in gaining social clout. Social clout is vital to them because they can use it to tilt the brand experience in their favor. For example, using their social clout to get upgrades on flights, rental cars and hotels.

13. Aversion to the sales pitch

Gone are the days when a simple "Buy Now!" sales pitch worked for the marketplace. This generation has been continually bombarded with ads from every media device possible and they're tired of it.

Don't try too hard to relate to them – they can tell if you are not being authentic. Millennials want real down-to-earth people who can truly connect with them and give them the truth. In short, they want authenticity to counteract their skepticism. Be consistent and transparent with whatever you tell them about your goods or services, and if their fact-checking reveals that you were right, they will be more eager to listen the next time.

An excellent way to sell to Millennials without sounding like a sales pitch is to offer them a unique experience, event, or particular offering. Sharing a sneak peek of something that's trending and timely also works.

14. Brand loyalty

How loyal are Millennials? With the assistance of social media, Millennials will spread the word about specific products or services they love, which leads to their impressive influential buying power of almost $1 trillion. That's a number you can't ignore.

Millennials spend up to 25 hours each week online, and when they find a product that they truly love, they are eager to post, tweet, and talk about it. Instead of paying for endorsements, opt for subscription and sampling services in your category. The upfront expenditure to build trials, authentic reviews, web traffic, and passion for your product is far less expensive than paying tens of thousands of dollars for one endorsement from a famous spokesperson. Millennials connect with each other and trust referrals from others within their network.

Millennials are not willing to be passive consumers; this generation wants to actively participate, co-create, and, most importantly, be included as partners in the brands they love. Driven by advances in digital and mobile technology, consumers of all ages can participate in these once closed-door processes, and many are accepting, if not demanding, the invitation.

For Millennials, it's almost an expectation that companies would want to seek them out for their opinion.

15. Convenience

Another effective loyalty-building strategy is to increase Millennials' connection to your brand by making it more fun, convenient, and relatable. They expect customer-centric shopping tailored to their needs and wants NOW, both online and in brick and mortar stores.

I had the privilege to partner with JCPenney to freshen their brand to connect with Millennials. As part of these changes, they're now offering more trend-setting brands to attract the Millennial consumer. JCPenney is eliminating cashiers, cash registers, and checkout counters and replacing them with technology-based self-checkout options that make checking out a breeze. Not surprisingly, Nordstrom Rack, a Millennial favorite, offers similar services.

16. Listen to them

Selling is no longer one-way communication. The fantastic thing about Millennials is that they WANT to engage in two-way communication with YOU – the brand, the business, or the cause they care about – and they're especially good at telling you what they love... and what they hate. If you're listening—truly listening—this can be incredibly helpful.

This may mean:

- Selling your products in starter or trial kits
- Using your customers as your models, so they feel like they are buying from a brand that represents them
- Asking them what new colors and styles they want to see
- Asking them where your next pop-up shop or event should be
- Asking them how they want you to communicate with them

Every decision made should be based on the feedback provided by your Millennial consumers, so when Millennials purchase, they are not just in love with the product, but they feel like they are a part of something special they helped to create.

17. Create loyalty by embracing a cause

We know through history that humans have an innate desire to be part of something bigger than themselves. Millennials are no different, and they push for this in the online and social space every day. It's critically important to organizations that Millennials know they are part of a much bigger movement and that they're with you in creating a more communal next-generation experience.

Millennials' purchasing habits tend to prioritize memorable experiences and social identity. They are more likely to embrace brands that are making a difference or supporting a cause they believe in. Millennials want to align themselves with organizations doing good in the world and they use their purchasing power to help companies that have similar values. Giving back to the animal community or the homeless have been favorite charities for this generation.

There may be advocacy that makes sense for your brand, like a toothpaste company helping underprivileged children get dentistry, or a home builder supporting Habitat for Humanity. If not, advocacy could come across as dubious or inauthentic. Instead, think of advocacy that you can see your company partnering with that matters to Millennials, and just subtly let them know that you can help them fight for their cause. If advocacies are not doable for you right now, share memorable memes and give them stories that will touch their hearts.

18. Stimulate brand loyalty through customer service

Customer service can also make or break brand loyalty. Social media has proven to be a useful tool for customer service. In fact, 64 percent of Millennial consumers believe that social media is one of the most effective channels for reaching brands.

Having your organization's customer service commitment online not only increases loyalty but it can keep customers coming back. Sixty-five percent of Millennials start interactions with a brand or an organization online.

To build loyalty among Millennial consumers, you must stand out from your competition and be the first to engage with Millennials and seek their feedback and insights. In addition to responding to customers' input by answering their questions and engaging with them on social media, prove to them that you care by acting on their insights. Not only will this show the Millennials you are actually listening, but that you are committed to enhancing your product and service offering.

19. Don't do social spamming

When it comes to engagement in social media, timing is the key. You need to make some noise to get your target market's eyeballs. Likewise, you need to do it wisely while competing with thousands of brands all similarly vying for the same Millennial audience's attention.

Instead of posting new content every hour, do something remarkable by engaging your audience in a conversation. Listen to what they are saying and respond timely to their comments and questions. One way to keep your company updated whenever somebody posts content about your brand online is to set up Google alerts. You can also eavesdrop on your competitors by setting up alarms whenever people mention their brands or products.

20. Cultivate exclusivity

Instead of peddling your wares all over the Millennial marketplace, turn the tables around and let them qualify themselves first, before they get your product. Make sure you are clear about your offering and state that it is only for highly qualified people. You can screen them using Google forms or surveys. You can also provide an ascending level of service depending on how well each person qualifies. This is one of the best ways to offer specialized service and high-ticket products to a small set of people inside your group without alienating the rest of your community. Think of it like developing your own "VIP Groupon."

21. Keep an eye and ear out for interesting stories

What do Michael Jordan's crying scene, Barack Obama's memes, Donald Trump's tweets, Kim Kardashian's butt, Caitlyn Jenner's transformation and the ice bucket challenge all have in common? They are all snippets of exciting stories that broke the Internet. Good brands should be like expert surfers, they must know how to ride a big wave. Likewise, as marketers to Millennials, you must be able to spot it a mile away. Depending on your product and market, ride on a recent trending story while it's hot. Connect your offer to the unique story and post it out there for your audience to see. Remember to use the right hashtag that is related to the story or movement.

Chapter Five

Portraits of the Five Generations

In America, there are at least five living generations, which are five distinct groups of people. As a generalization each generation has different likes, dislikes, and attributes. They have had collective experiences as they've aged and therefore have similar ideals.

A person's birthdate may not always be indicative of their generational characteristics, but as a common group they have similarities. This knowledge can be helpful when creating consumer marketing strategies.

MEET THE GENERATIONS

Traditionalists: Born 1922 – 1944

Baby Boomers: Born 1945 – 1964

Generation X: Born 1965 – 1979

Millennials: Born 1980 – 1996

Generation Z: Born 1997 and Later

Traditionalists: Born 1922 – 1944

- Values privacy, trust, hard work
- Believes in paying their dues
- Respects authority and social order
- Conformists, historically orientated, loyal
- Needs details, uncomfortable with ambiguity
- Grew up in a manufacturing era where physical labor and assembly line work were more common and rewarded than knowledge capital
- Prefers personal contact and connection, or a live person versus a telephone call or email
- Tends to be wary of new technology and may find it intimidating and confusing to learn ATM's, voicemail, etc.

Baby Boomers: Born 1945 – 1964

- Majority of today's workers
- Loves to be challenged
- First generation of TV addicts
- Speaks clearly and directly
- Likes face-to-face meetings with follow up emails
- Seeks the career-ladder development
- The rise of television transformed their social habits
- In the forefront of creating digital revolutions; 70's technological revolution was beginning to replace manufacturing as the core of the economy
- Technology is important to the current lifestyle at work and home but is a challenge to learn

Generation X: Born 1965 – 1979

- Looks for a leader or mentor, not necessarily a boss
- Embraces diversity and inclusion
- Technology literate - the first generation to grow up with VCR's, personal PC's, video games, and MTV
- Grew up in an environment of instant information such as open investigative reporting on TV and access to any type of information via the Internet
- More educated than previous generations
- Values portable careers and doesn't believe in climbing ladders
- Looks for a chance to go global

Millennials: Born 1980 – 1996

- Generation "Why"
- Children of Baby Boomers
- Talented and a hot commodity in the job market
- Higher expectations with little experience
- Multitaskers, confident and loyal
- Creates a "lattice framework" of experience
- Hyper aware of branding & marketing that isn't authentic
- Wants to live their life NOW not later
- Grew up surrounded by digital media and are more comfortable, knowledgeable, and device-literate than prior generations
- Use of technology has created demands for instant gratification
- Customizes their digital world as new products come onto the market
- Extensive on-line users who can locate information easily and instantly on the Internet and through social networking

Generation Z: Born 1997 and Later

- Multitaskers at warp speed, prefers to work on five screens at a time

- Requires connectivity between home, school & life

- Realistic and cynical, not idealistic

- Passionate about learning

- Financially diligent about preparing for the future

- Private when sharing on social media

- Entrepreneurial, they want to be pioneers and don't want to settle for a "career"

- They are hyper-aware of their surroundings at work and home

- They are technology-reliant, putting technology in the same category as air and water

Conclusion

Generational diversity and inclusion are critical elements to finding success in every layer of society within our ever-changing world. Within every generation, there are those who embrace the new and look for ways to engage and understand changing methodologies, and those who reject anything that is different.

Everyone has a choice to make. You can be open-minded to the inevitable changes that appear with every new generation or you can be close-minded to new trends and strategies and get left behind.

Diversity helps businesses thrive, and Millennials are the most diverse generation in history. It is important to understand that Millennial diversity does not simply mean race and ethnicity, it also includes family backgrounds.

More so than previous generations, the majority of Millennials come from single-parent homes, same-sex families, and blended families. When you consider their dynamic and diverse experiences, it will help you develop better strategies to reach them as consumers.

Why are Millennials so important? Because they are defining trends and disrupting markets. When you can **Crack the Millennial Code** and effectively connect with Millennials in a meaningful manner, you will have access to their world of diversity and inclusion and gain their loyalty as a fan and consumer.

What's Next

Crack the Millennial Code: Strategies to Market to Millennials, is the first book in a three-part series. The next two books in this series discuss strategies that will help you tap into the incredible talent pool of Millennials and will provide you with proven techniques for managing and motivating them, so you can harness their power.

Here's a sample of what the next two books will offer, which will be especially helpful to those who are looking to **Crack the Millennial Code**.

For Millennials:

- *"Loving what I do" is among the top options for job desirability, outranking salaries and big bonuses.*
- *Each day they devote 5.4 hours to social media & they check their smartphones 43 times.*
- *30% plan to leave their job in the next year.*
- *43% said they are open to offers.*
- *91% expect to stay at a job for less than three years.*
- *81% want more flexible work schedules.*
- *They are the most ethnically diverse generation & the most educated generation.*

To reach Millennials and achieve better results, your strategies must connect with their habits, desires, passions, and preferences.

What has historically worked in the past for peers or older generations is no longer relevant when looking to reach a younger demographic.

To help with your assessment of their skills, and to determine if their attitude towards the job at hand is compatible with the job description, here are three questions to ask during an interview:

Question 1: *Have you ever had to wear a uniform, cover up a tattoo, or work at a time that was difficult for you, like early in the morning or late at night? How did you handle that?*

The candidate's response will give insight into how they coped with a task that required them to compromise personal style or conform to standards they disagreed with.

Follow up by discussing the most unpleasant aspects of the job, whether it involves grunt work or dealing with rude customers. Someone who still wants the job after hearing the negatives is more likely to last in the position.

Question 2: *What do you read or listen to every day to get the news?*

The answer to this question reveals the candidate's curiosity and interest in the broader world. Do they read anything beyond Buzzfeed and Twitter?

Question 3: *What kind of relationship do you expect to have with your boss?*

Millennials may have never had a formal relationship with a boss. This interview question prevents mismatched expectations. Millennials want people to be friendly with them. Working for you may be the first time they have a relationship with an authority figure they don't perceive as being friendly.

You do not want to miss the next two books in this series. Go to *GenerationalGuru.com* for more information.

Need Help Managing Millennials?

Check out Book 2,
***Crack the Millennial Code:
Strategies to Manage Millennials***

For more information about this book,
to order, and for additional resources, go to
CrackTheMillennialCode.com.

Need Help Motivating Millennials?

Check out Book 3,
Crack the Millennial Code: Strategies to Motivate Millennials

For more information about this book,
to order, and for additional resources, go to
CrackTheMillennialCode.com.

About the Author

Sherri Elliott-Yeary, CEO of Generational Guru, is an award-winning speaker, professional business consultant, and published author who energetically engages international audiences with her practical strategies for attracting, growing, and retaining top talent and loyal customers from every generation. Sherri brings over twenty years of hands-on experience to support you in designing generational solutions that address:

- Cross-Generational Leadership Challenges

- Generational Blind Spots in Sales

- Recruitment & Retention

- Marketing & Communicating with Millennials

- Reverse Mentoring

- Knowledge Capital Transfer

Sherri has provided training and support on generational issues to thousands of leaders and major professional associations across the US, UK, and Canada. Sherri's books, articles, podcasts, training, and consulting explain how generational misunderstandings affect every aspect of a business, including recruitment and retention, management, generational research, motivation, and sales and marketing.

Sherri's unique inter-generational approach integrates the critical elements of communication, sociology, business psychology, and demography to connect workplaces and dramatically improve company performance and sales.

She is passionately committed to helping organizations achieve higher productivity, increased morale, and better retention rates. Sherri offers her clients practical solutions and lessons on improving communication, so they can solve the generational issues that confront their specific industries. She has provided generational insight and advice to the nation's most prominent corporations, including Chevron, Nissan, Pepsi Co., the National Guard, Frito-Lay, Christus Health, Raytheon, Bank of America, GameStop, Citibank, and Marriott International.

Sherri lives in Dallas, Texas, with her husband and sassy dog, Coco. Their three Millennial daughters have successfully launched and are living life on their terms!

You can learn more about Sherri and the programs she offers at **www.generationalguru.com** and **www.sharingwithsher.com**.

You can also connect with Sherri on Facebook, Instagram, Twitter, LinkedIn, Pinterest, and YouTube. Her podcast, **Sharing with Sher**, can be found on iTunes, Sound Cloud, and Apple Podcasts.

"A mind that is stretched by a new experience can never go back to its old dimensions."

—Oliver Wendell Holmes, Jr.